Copyright @ 2014
All rights reserved. No part of this publication may be reproduced by any means without permission in writing from the publisher..

Printed in the United States of America

Machine Knitting Resource Book

by
Joyce Bragdon

This book is dedicated
to my awesome kids,

Christopher
and
Roxanne

who keep me

Thinking,
Creating
and Living

Table of Contents

PART 1

Abbreviations	11
Charted Symbols	15
Conversion Charts	17
Get to know your machine	19
What yarn do I use?	23
Yarn chart	27
Weight Class	29
Yarn estimates	33
Yarn Resources	35
Burn Test	37
Size Charts	39
Explanation of terms.	53
Basic functions	55

PART 2

Let's Knit !!! …….swatches	59
The cartridge, cam, controls, tension	61
Casting on	65
Binding off	73
Punch cards	75
Troubleshooting	77
Resources	79

Hello and welcome.

"Machine Knitting Resource Book" was written from many hours of frustration, note-taking and tutorials. I was so excited to receive my knitting machine, and lo and behold saw this crazy thing in front of me and didn't know where to start.

I found that it actually wasn't that hard to figure out, and with a bit of patience and *LOTS* of help from all over the web, it all made perfect sense.

It would have been so much easier if I knew where to go for all this information in the first place.

As you read this book, you will see, it is mainly a compilation of *GREAT* sites and information that took me way too long to find and bookmark.

Everything, now, finally at my (and your) fingertips to use again and again as you practice, as you start a garment or as you start your own designs.......

This book does contain some basic instructions. In case you are missing a manual or are having trouble finding one, (there is a resource listed). That way, at least you can start to have some fun right away!

Have fun.

Joyce

Knitting Machine Abbreviations

Understanding the terminology for machine knitting is important for the understanding of written patterns made for machine knitters.

Below you will find a list of terms suitable for most Japanese knitting machines referenced to quite frequently in most popular machine knitting publications.

Please note that some symbols have more than one definition and is defined by its context.

A	first contrast color used
A/H	Armhole
Alt	alternate
Alt	alternate(ly)
B	second contrast color used
BH	buttonhole
BB	back bed
Beg	beginning
BET	between
BK	back
BO	bind off
BOLT	Slip Stitch bind off with a latch tool
C off	cast off
C on	cast on
C	third contrast color used
CAL	carriage on left
CAR	carriage on right
Carr	carriage
CC	contrast color
Cm	centimeters
CO	cast on
COBH	cast on by hand
Col	color
Con	contrast
CONT	continue

Cont	continue
DB	double bed
DEC	(dec) decrease
DECR	two stitches to the next two needles
DK	double knit
E/N	every needle
E/R	every row
EON	ever other needle
EOR	every other row
EOST	every other stitch
Ev	(ev) every
FA	feeder A
FB	feeder B
Ff	(FF) fully fashioned
FNP	first needle position
FNR	full needle rib
Foll	(foll) following
G	(gm) grams
G.B.	(G bar) garter bar
GC	garter carriage
H	hold
HP	half pitch
HP	hold position
In(s)	inch(es)
Inc	increase
INC	increase
K	knit
KH	main bed (knitting carriage)
K carriage	knitting carriage
KWK	knit across, wrap, knit back
LHS	left hand side
LPC	lock punch card
M	main color
MB	main bed
MC	main color
Mm	millimeters
MT	main tension
N	needle(s)
NB	needle bed

ND	neck
NDL	needle
ndl(s)	needles(s)
Ndls	needles
NWP	non-working position
OPP	(opp) opposite
OWP	out of work position
Oz	ounces
P	(Pl) Plain
P	purl
patt(s)	patterns
PC	punch card
PK	partial knit
Pl	(P) plain
PM	place marker
PU	pick up
RB	ribber bed
RC	row counter
Rem	remaining
Rep	repeat
RH	rehang
RHS	right hand side
RP	rest position
RPc	release punch card
RS	right side
RT	rib tension
S/R	short rows
SR	short row
SB	single bed
SD	stitch dial
SH	shoulder
SHR	short row
Sl	slip

SR	(SHR) short row
SS	stitch tension
St st	stocking stitch
St(s)	stitch(es)
ST-RS-X'S	stitches-rows-times
st-st	stocking stitch
T	tension
TD	tension dial
TEN	tension
Tog	together
TR	turning row
Trans	(trans) transfer
UWP	upper working position
W	work
WP	work position
Ws	wrong side
WY	waste yarn
X	times
YF	yarn feeder
YM	yarn marker
YO	yarn over

Charting Symbols

Hand manipulation requires you to work certain stitches by hand to create a desired pattern. A design is "charted" line by line with these symbols

.

Symbol/Name	How to Work			
Knit Stitch |	Face loop of plain stitch			
Purl Stitch —	Back loop of Plain stitch			
Hole O	Transfer Stitch to Next needle			
Two stitches together ⋋	Transfer right Stitch to adjacent Left needle			
Two stitches together ⋌	Transfer left Stitch to adjacent right needle			
Three stitches together ⋏	Center stitch on Top of left and Right stitches			
Three stitches together ⋋	Right stitch on top			
Three stitches together ⋌	Left stitch on top			
Lean stitch to right /	Left stitch To right			
Lean stitch to left \	Right stitch To left			

Symbol/Name   How to Work

Symbol/Name	How to Work			
Increased stitch to right ᖉ	Increase one stitch To left			
Increased stitch to left ᖌ	Increase one stitch To left			
Three stitch increase V³	The loops Made by Winding the wool Around the needles			
Crossing. Right Over the left ✕	Cross the stitches, right stitch over the left			
Crossing, left Over the right ✕	Cross the stitches left stitch over the right			
Cross stitch through left stitch ⤬	Crossed stitches with right side stitch through stitch on left side			
Cross stitch through Right stitch ⤫	Crossed stitches with left side stitch through stitch on right side			
Slip stitch V	A loop marked is pulled up with yarn across behind it			
Float stitch ∀	A loop marked is pulled up with yarn across in the front			
Tuck stitch ∩	A few loops on marked rows pulled up onto one needle			
Twisted tuck stitch ᛆ	A stitch twisted and pulled up onto a needle above			
Twisted stitch ȣ	Stitch is twisted			
Winding stitch ω	The loops made by winding the wool around the needles			

Conversion Charts

Standard Lengths and Weights

1 inch = 2.54 centimeters
1 yard = 0.91 meter
2 centimeters- = 0.79 inches
5 centimeters = 1.97 inches
1 meter = 1.09 yards
2 ounces = 56.7 grams
50 grams = 1.75 ounces

Conversion Formulas

Multiply by	To Convert	To
2.54	inches	centimeters
30.48	feet	centimeters
0.9144	yards	meters
6.452	sq. inches	sq. centimeters
28.35	ounces	grams
0.4536	pounds	kilograms
0.3937	centimeters	inches
0.0328	centimeters	feet
0.000621	meters	yards
0.155	sq. centimeters	sq. inches
0.0352	grams	ounces
2.2045	kilograms	pounds

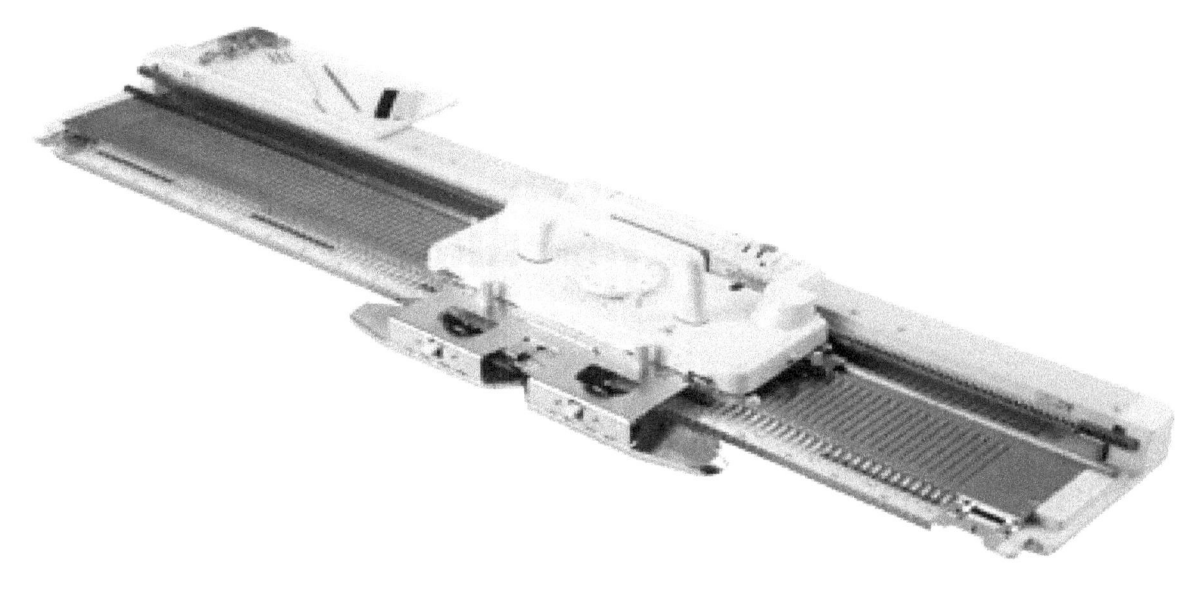

Getting to know your machine

Whenever we get a new toy, of course we want to jump right in and use it. That's what I do. I bought a vintage machine on ebay and while I was waiting for it, watched every youtube video and searched every website I could find…..

As you're waiting for your machine to arrive,

Download an instruction book for you model and print it for visual use. If you are buying or have bought a vintage, and most are, don't expect the manual. Considering most machines are 10+ years or older, (mine is 1998), manuals get lost or just unreadable.

Sites for FREE manuals...and more:

http://machineknittingetc.com/
http://knittsings.com/knitting-machine-manuals/
http://www.andeeknits.co.uk/

ALSO........

Buy a new sponge bar (or 2).

If you receive your knitting machine with an old flat bar, your needles will loop over the yarn, skip or drop. Flat bed knitting machines need a sponge bar that is fresh and springy to hold the needles in place for the carriage to run smoothly back and forth. It is about 3/8" wide and runs the length of the bed. It may also be called the needle retaining bar. Also, many ribbers also require one, so check that too, if you bought one.

You can buy them here:

http://spongebar.com/
http://www.theknittingcloset.com/cat-sponge-barsneedle-retainer-bars.cfm
http://www.xenaknits.com/

Here is a good site to read about them:

http://knittsings.com/knitting-machine-sponge-bar/

If you know you are not going to use the machine for an extended period of time, it is a good idea to slide the bar out to rest.

YARNS

What yarn do I use?

You do not need special yarns…!!!!

And

There are so many yarns out there……..

Yarn on cones are my favorite and are available on so many places on the internet now. It is easy to pick up one for $10 to experiment. There are also fabulous yarns in hanks and balls.

But…you MUST know your machine. I know I cannot use any bulky yarns even if I use every other needle. The needle just splits the yarn and I end up with a mess…….well, I tried.

Don't be afraid to experiment. Spend the first couple of sittings, just playing. Get the feel of the carriage gliding back and forth. Change the tension. Teach your self to cast on and to bind off

Yarns that are NOT GOOD are nubby, metallic or sequince. As you practice, it will then seem obvious to you. The yarn you choose needs to glide easily past the thread tension arm, through the carriage and be able to lay across the needle bed. If there are any irregularities (sequince or knubs) you may miss or drop stitches, bend a needle or even worse - get your carriage stuck in the middle of your work. UGH!

With that said…..you will find that you CAN work with these yarns if you weave then in by hand, then carefully push the carriage over them.

Needle spacing and hook size are important factors. Passap knitting machines have needles spaced at 3, 5 and 10 mm. Brother and KnitKing machines are available in 3.5 or 3.6 mm (fine gauge), 4.5 mm (standard gauge) and 9.0 mm (bulky gauge). Some other knitting machines are available in 6.5, 7.0 and 8.0 mm and are called Mid Gauge machines.

However, you may be able to expand a bit past those gauges. It may be possible to knit heavier yarns on a smaller gauge machine. The trick is to use every other needle, or even every third needle. Beware not to push what it cannot handle, too heavy of a yarn may cause extensive problems. Experiment with care.

Knitting machines come in various gauges to accommodate the wide range of yarns available today. Use the following chart to approximate what yarns are best for you. Of course there are always variables with gauges and stitches per inch. Also lace weight and fingering weight yarns are often knit on looser tension for openwork patterns.

YARN CHART

Below is a quick guide to gauges, yarns and how they are sold per cones. As you browse the chart, you can see how some yarns may be able to "crossover".

Fine Gauge 3,6mm

    Lace weight 32-36 st/4 inches
    Light Fingering 32-36 st/4 inches

    3000-6000 yards/ pound

Standard Gauge 4.5mm

    Baby weight 27-32 st/4 inches

    2400-3000yards/ pound

    Fingering 27-32 st/4 inches

    1800-2400yards/ pound

    Sock weight 27-32 st/4 inches

    1800-2400yards/ pound

Mid-Gauge 6-7mm

> **Sport weight** 21-26st/4 inches
>
> 1300-1800yards/ pound
>
> **DK (Double Knit)** 21-26st/4 inches
>
> 1000-1400yards/pound
>
> **Light worsted** 21-26st/4 inches
>
> 900-1100yards/ pound
>
> **Aran** 16-20 st/4 inches
>
> 700-1000yards/ pound
>
> **Afghan** 16-20 st/4 inches
>
> 700-1000yards/ pound

Bulky/Chunky 8-9

> **Handspun** 12-15 st/4 inches
>
> 400-700yards/ pound
>
> **Bulky** 12-15 st/4 inches
>
> 400-700yards/ pound
>
> **Heavy worsted** 12-15 st/4 inches
> Varies
>
> **Super Bulky** 8-12 st/4 inches
> Varies

Yarn by Weight Class and General Terms

Light FINGERING 10-COUNT CROCHET THREAD…The lightest weight of yarn. Used to make lace, doilies and other delicate items.

FINGERING WEIGHT: SOCK, FINGERING, BABY YARN…A very lightweight yarn used for baby wear, socks, and other delicate items. Beautiful for Fair Isle. UK/Australia approximate equivalent: 3 ply, 4 ply, 5 ply, jumper weight
Sometimes listed as "Baby Yarn".

SPORT WEIGHT: FINE, SPORT WEIGHT, BABY YARN…A light weight yarn used for baby wear, sweaters, and lighter throws. UK/Australia approximate equivalent: 8 ply

LIGHT WORSTED YARN: DK WEIGHT Used for baby and light-weight adult garments. UK/Australia approximate equivalent: DK (Double Knit)   Sport weight yarn and DK (double knitting) weight yarn are often viewed as interchangeable, but they do have a slight difference. Sport weight yarn is slightly lighter or finer than DK weight. Note: the word 'sport' is meant for women's *sport*swear. Use these weights for socks, accessories, shawls, wraps, and heirloom.

WORSTED WEIGHT: AFGHAN, ARAN YARN
The most popular weight for knitting and crocheting. An ideal weight for throws and many adult garments. UK/Australia approximate equivalent: 10 ply, Aran weight

Worsted weight yarn is the most widely available weight of yarn and the most frequently used. At double the weight of fingering yarn, worsted weight yarn is great for knitters of all skill levels and can be worked into nearly anything.

HEAVY WORSTED WEIGHT: is another popular yarn, and yes, heavier than the worsted weight. Good for the same range of projects as worsted weight.

BULKY WEIGHT: CHUNKY, CRAFT, RUG YARN
About twice as thick worsted weight, bulky yarn works up quickly and easily for such things as hats, scarves, sweaters, pillows and throws. UK/Australia approximate equivalent: 13 ply

SUPER BULKY WEIGHT: BULKY, ROVING YARN
A very heavy yarn, Super bulky is the ultimate for making fast knits. Projects work up extremely fast. UK/Australia approximate equivalent: 14 ply

SWEATER EASE ALLOWANCE

Very Close Fit – minus 2"
Close Fit – Actual Measurements
Normal Fit – add 2"
Loose Fit – add 4"
Oversized – add more than 4"

How Much ease should I add? This is a very personal decision. The chart above gives the general amounts allowed for different types of fit. However, inch amounts alone are not the total answer. You must create a swatch with the yarn you will be using. Wash and dry if you want it washable. Then check your gauge not only for stitches, but for stretchability.

I usually make an 8 x 8 inch swatch, then thread a tapestry needle with thick thread of a contrast color, and sewing through the knit loops, mark out a 6 x 6 area. After it is dry, lay it out on a flat surface then stretch it across a ruler. If it is firm, you may need a bit of ease. If it stretches freely, you may need less. If your still not sure, make a larger swatch and stretch it across your body.

One of the best tips is to measure a favorite sweater, taking note of the weight and type of fabric. Most pullover sweaters, which are meant to be worn in place of a blouse or shirt, include 2-4" ease at the chest.

Yardage Estimates for Sweaters, Pullovers or Cardigans

The following guidelines are for the amounts of yarn needed for a basic pullover or cardigan in a variety of sizes and yarn sizes. These estimates are for smooth yarns and plain or lightly textured knitting. Allow for two colors or double textured designs.

If you run out and need more, the dye lots may not match. Always be generous!

Babies 12-18 Months

fingering weight: 600-700 yards (550-650 meters)
sportweight: 550-650 yards (500-600 meters)
worsted weight: 450-550 (400-500 meters)

Toddlers 2-6 Years

sportweight: 800-1000 yards (750-950 meters)
worsted weight: 600-800 yards (550-750 meters)
bulky weight: 550-650 yards (500-600 meters)

Children 6-12 Years

sportweight: 1000-1500 yards (950-1400 meters)
worsted weight: 900-1200 yards (850-1100 meters)
bulky weight: 700-1000 yards (650-950 meters)

Misses Sizes 32-40 Bust

fingering weight: 1500-1700yards (1400-1600 meters)
sportweight: 1400-1600 yards (1300-1500 meters)
worsted weight: 1100-1400 yards (1000-1300 meters)
bulky weight: 1000-1300 yards (950-1200 meters)
sportweight: 1500-1900 yards (1400-1750 meters)
worsted weight: 1300-1500 yards (1200-1400 meters)
bulky weight: 1100-1400 yards (1000-1300 meters)
    --add 5% for longer or looser fit
    --add 5% for cardigan

Misses Sizes 42-50 Bust

sportweight: 1600-2000 yards (1500-1850 meters)
worsted weight: 1400-1600 yards (1300-1500 meters)
bulky weight: 1200-1400 yards (1100-1300 meters)
    --add 5% for cardigan

Men sizes 36-48 Chest

sportweight: 1700-2100 yards (1600-1950 meters)
worsted weight: 1500-1700 yards (1400-1600 meters)
bulky weight: 1300-1500 yards (1200-1400 meters)
sportweight: 2000-2400 yards (1850-2200 meters)
worsted weight: 1500-1700 yards (1650-1850 meters)
bulky weight: 1300-1500 yards (1400-1550 meters)
    --add 5% for longer or looser fit
    --add 5% for cardigan

Some places to try for yarn:

Please note: I do not endorse any of these shops.
I have shopped at many of these stores, and others were referrals. All sites are live at time of this writing.

amazon.com

ebay.com
etsy.com

http://www.deramores.com

http://jimmybeanswool.com
http://yarn.com
http://yarnmarket.com
http://Lionbrand.com
http://store.knitting-warehouse.com/

http://www.herrschners.com

http://www.yeoman-yarns.co.uk

http://www.anniescatalog.com/yarn_and_thread/index.html

http://smileysyarns.com

http://www.knitpicks.com
http://www.yarn-paradise.com/
http://www.aboutknittingmachines.com/
   KnittingMachineYarn.php

Burn Test
Fiber Identification

When trying to identify an unknown yarn fiber, burning a few inches of the yarn could sometimes help to identify the fiber content of the yarn. The following are some various characteristics of burning yarn:

Cotton: Burns rapidly, yellow flames, continues burning; afterglow. Smells like paper. Residue is a brown tinged end, feathery ash

Linen Burns slower than cotton; afterglow. Smells like rope. Ash maintains shape of swatch.

Ramie Burns slowly. Smells like rope. Ash maintains shape of swatch.

Rayon Burns slowly. Smells like paper or rags. Very little residue, fluffy ash.

Silk and Wool Burns slowly, Usually self-extinguishing. Smells like hair. Residue is crushable black bead (silk) or small, brittle, black bead (wool).

Most synthetic fibers Nylon, polyester, acrylic, tend to melt and fuse. Nylon and polyester leave a hard, gray or tan bead; acrylic will leave a crisp, black mass.

SIZE CHART

NATIONAL STANDARD

Size charts can be confusing. About 20 or so years ago a clothing designer decided he would sell his clothes "dropping" a size. Another words, if you wore a size 12, in his clothes you would now wear a 10. It caught on and most designers use this "new" sizing. However, there are still designers that use the National Standard, such as bridal.

As you work with patterns….
use the measurements, not sizing.

MISSES' STANDARD SIZE CHART
All Measurements in Inches

Size	6	8	10	12	14
Bust	31.5	32.5	33.5	35	36.5
Waist	23	24	25	26.5	28
Hip	33.5	34.5	35.5	37	38.5
Back Width	13	13.5	14	14.5	15
Neck Width	4	4	4.5	4.5	5
Each Shoulder	4.5	4.75	4.75	5	5
Back Waist Length	15	15.25	15.5	15.75	16
Armhole Depth	7	7.25	7.25	7.5	7.5
Upper Arm	9.75	10	10.25	10.5	11
Wrist	5.5	5.75	6	6.25	6.5
Sleeve Seam Length	16.5	16.75	17	17.5	17.75

MISSES' STANDARD SIZE CHART
(continued)

Size	16	18	20	22
Bust	38	40	42	44
Waist	30	32	34	36
Hip	40	42	44	46
Back Width	15.5	16	16.5	17
Neck Width	5	5.5	5.5	5.5
Each Shoulder	5.25	5.25	5.5	5.75
Back Waist Length	16.25	16.5	16.75	17
Armhole Depth	7.75	7.75	8	8
Upper Arm	11.5	12	12.5	13
Wrist	6.75	7	7.5	8
Sleeve Seam Length	18	18	18	18

Baby's size

	3 Months	6 M	12 M	18 M	24 M
Chest (in.)	16	17	18	19	20
(cm)	40.5	43	45.5	48	50.5
Waist	18	19	20	20	21
	45.5	48	50.5	52	53.5
Hips	19	20	20	21	22
	48	50.5	50.5	53.5	56
Center Back Neck-to-Cuff	10	11	12	14	18
	26.5	29	31.5	35.5	45.5
Back Waist Length	6	7	7	8	8
	15.5	17.5	19	20.5	21.5
Shoulder to Shoulder	7	7	8	8	8
	18.5	19.5	21	21.5	22
Sleeve Length to Underarm	6	6	7	8	8
	15.5	16.5	19	20.5	21.5
Upper arm	5	6	6	7	7
	14	15.5	16.5	17.5	19
Armhole depth	3	3	3	4	4
	8.5	9	9.5	10	10.5
Neck Width	3.25	3.25	3.5	3.5	3.75
	7.25	7.25	8.75	8.75	9.25
Head	15	16	17	18	19
	37.5	40	42.5	4	47.5
Wrist	4.75	5	5	5.25	5.5
	11.75	12.5	12.5	13.25	13.75

Children size 2 – 5

Size	2	3	4	5
Chest	21	22	23	24
Waist	20	20.75	21.5	22.5
Hip	22	23	24	25
Back ……Width	8.75	9	9.5	10
Neck ……Width	3.5	3.5	3.75	3.75
Each Shoulder.	2.625	2.75	2.875	3.125
Back …….Waist ….Length	8	8.75	9.5	10.5
Armhole ……..Depth	4	4.25	4.5	4.75
Upper …..Arm	7.25	7.5	7.75	8
Wrist	5.25	5.25	5.5	5.5
Sleeve …….Seam ……Length	8.5	9.5	10.5	11.5
Head	18	19	19.5	20

Children size 6 – 12

Size	6	8	10	12
Chest	25	27	29	31
Waist	23.5	25	26	27
Hip	26	28.5	31	33
Back Width	10.5	11	11.5	12
Neck Width	3.75	4	4	4
Each Shoulder	3.375	3.5	3.75	4
Back Waist Length	11.5	12.5	13.5	14.5
Armhole Depth	5	5.5	6	6.5
Upper Arm	8.25	8.5	8.75	9
Wrist	5.75	5.75	6	6
Sleeve Seam Length	12.5	13.5	14.5	15.5
Head	20.5	21	21.5	22

MEN'S SIZE CHARTS

All Measurements in Inches

Size	32	34	36	38	40	52
Chest	32	34	36	38	40	52
Waist	26	28	30	32	34	50
Hip	33	35	37	39	41	53
Back Width	15	15.5	16	16.5	17	20
Neck Width	5	5.25	5.25	5.5	5.75	7
Each Shoulder	5	5.25	5.35	5.5	5.7	6.5
Back Waist Length	15	15.25	15.5	15.75	16	17.5
Armhole Depth	7	7.25	7.5	8	8.25	10.5
Upper Arm	10	10.5	11	11.5	12	16
Wrist	6	6.25	6.5	6.75	7	9.5
Sleeve Seam Length	18	18.25	18.5	18.75	19	20.5

MEN'S SIZE CHARTS

All Measurements in Inches

Size	44	46	48	50	52	54
Chest	44	46	48	50	52	54
Waist	39	42	44	47	50	52
Hip	45	47	49	51	53	55
Back Width	18	18.5	19	19.5	20	20.5
Neck Width	6	6	6.5	6.5	7	7
Each Shoulder	6	6.25	6.26	6.5	6.5	6.75
Back Waist Length	16.5	16.75	17	17.25	17.5	17.75
Armhole Depth	8.75	9	9.5	10	10.5	11
Upper Arm	13	13.5	14	15	16	17
Wrist	7.5	8	8.5	9	9.5	10
Sleeve Seam Length	19.5	19.75	20	20.25	20.5	20.75

Misses Ready to Wear - Size Chart

These measurements are closest to current US sizing

Size	2	4	6	8	10	12
Bust	32	33	34	35	36	37.5
Waist	24	25	26	27	28	29.5
Hip	34.5	35.5	36.5	37.5	38.5	40
Back Width	13.5	13.75	14	14.25	14.5	15
Back Neck	4.5	4.5	4.75	4.75	5	5
Armhole Depth	7	7.25	7.25	7.5	7.5	7.75
Back Waist Length	14.5	14.75	15	15.25	15.5	15.75
Upper Arm Width	9	9.25	9.5	9.75	10	10.5
Wrist width	6	6	6	6.25	6.5	6.75
Sleeve Seam Length	16	16.25	16.5	16.75	17	17.25
Shoulder Slope	1	1	1	1	1.25	1.25
Head Girth	21	21	21.25	21.25	21.5	21.75
Neck Girth	12	12.5	13	13.5	14	14.5
Waist-Hip	7	7	7.25	7.5	7.75	8
Waist-Knee	22	22.25	22.5	22.75	23	23.5
Crotch Depth	9.5	9.75	10	10.25	10.5	10.75

Misses Ready to Wear - Size Chart

These measurements are closest to current US sizing

Size	14	16	18	20	22	24
Bust	39	40.5	42.5	44.5	47	49.5
Waist	31	32.5	34.5	36.5	38.5	42.5
Hip	41.5	43	45	47	49	52
Back Width	15.5	16	16.5	17	17.5	18
Back Neck	5.25	5.25	5.5	5.5	5.75	5.75
Armhole Depth	7.75	8	8	8.25	8.5	8.75
Back Waist Length	16	16.25	16.5	16.75	17	17.25
Upper Arm Width	11	11.5	12	13	14	15
Wrist width	7	7.25	7.5	7.75	8	8.25
Sleeve Seam Length	17.5	17.75	18	18.25	18.5	18.75
Shoulder Slope	1.25	1.25	1.5	1.5	1.5	1.5
Head Girth	22	22.25	22.5	22.75	23	23.5
Neck Girth	15	15.5	16	16.5	17	17.5
Waist-Hip	8.25	8.5	8.75	9	9.25	9.5
Waist-Knee	24	24.5	25	25.5	26	26.5
Crotch Depth	11	11.25	11.5	11.75	12	12.25

Women shown in centimeters

Bust	81.5	86.5	91.5	96.5	101.5	106.5
Finished measurement	86.5	91.5	96.5	101.5	106.5	112.0
Hips	81.5	86.5	91.5	96.5	101.5	106.5
Hips Finished	91.5	96.5	101.5	106.5	112.0	117.0

Length from the back neck

Sweater	53.5	55.0	56.0	57.0	58.5	60.0
Cardigan	55.0	56.0	57.0	58.5	60.0	61.0
Sleeve length (long)	42.0	43.0	44.0	46.0	47.0	48.5
Armhole depth	16.0	18.0	19.0	20.5	22.0	23.0
Upper arm	30.5	32.0	33.0	34.0	35.5	37.0
Wrist	20.5	21.0	22.0	22.5	23.0	23.5
Back neck	13.0	14.0	14.5	15.0	15.5	16.0
Shoulder to shoulder	33.0	34.0	35.5	37.0	38.0	39.0
Shoulder slope	2.5					
Neck depth without band	7.5					

HATS

	Circumference		Length (crown to base of ear)	
	inches	cm	inches	cm
Preemie	12	30.5	4.25	11
Newborn	14	35.5	5	12.5
6 month	16	40.5	5.75	14.5
12 month	18	45.5	6.5	16.5
Child	20	50.5	7.25	18.5
Adult	22	56	8.25	21
Lg. Adult	24	61	9.25	23.5

Infants & Child Shoe Size Chart

Child's size (U.S. sizes)	0–4	4–8	7–11	10–2	2–6
Sock Size (U.S. sizes)	4–5	5–6½	6–7½	7–8½	8–9½
Ages	6–12 mo.	1–3 y.	3–5 y.	5–9 y.	7–13 y.
11a. Foot Circum. (in.)	4 ½	5 ½	6	6 ½	7
(cm.)	11	14	15.5	16.5	17.5
11b. Sock Height	2½	3½	4½	5½	6½
	6.5	9	11.5	14	16.5
11c. Total Foot Length	4	5	6	7½	8
	10	13	15.5	19	20.5

Woman Shoe Size Chart

Women's size (U.S. sizes)	3–6	6–9	8–12
Sock Size (U.S. sizes)	7–9	9–11	10–12
11a. Foot Circum. (in.)	7	8	9
(cm.)	17.5	20.5	23
11b. Sock Height	6½	7	7½
	16.5	17.5	19
11c. Total Foot Length	9	10	11
	23	25.5	28

Man Shoe Size Chart

Man size (U.S. sizes)	6–8	8½–10	10½–12	12½–14
Sock Size (U.S. sizes)	10	11	12	14
11a. Foot Circum. (in.)	7	8	9	10
(cm.)	17.5	20.5	23	25.5
11b. Sock Height	7	7½	8	8½
	17.5	19	20.5	21.5
11c. Total Foot Length	9½	10½	11	11½
	24	26.5	28	29

Machine Knitting Terms

Fine Gauge: Knitting machines with 3.6 or fewer mm needle pitch. Called 8 or higher cut.
Standard Gauge: Knitting machines with 5 mm or 4.5 mm needle pitch. Also known as 6 or 7 cut machines.
Bulky Gauge: Knitting machines with 9 or 10 mm needle pitch. Also known as 2 or 3 cut machines.
Cut: Generally means number of needles per inch on the needle bed.
Fair Isle: This is a type of knitting that originated in the Fair Isles near Great Britain. The term has come to mean any type of knitting that has a multiple color pattern knitted into the fabric.
Jacquard: A repeating pattern in knitting, usually using punch cards and can be a solid color. This is also referred to as Fair Isle knitting, but Fair Isle uses 2 or more colors.
Double Jacquard: This is Jacquard knitting on one face of a double knitted fabric.
Full Fashioned: Knitting that is shaped during the knitting process so that the finished piece has bound off edges on all sides.
Single Bed: This is a flat bed of needles. It produces jersey, or stocking stitch knitting. Some single bed machines have the ability to knit Fair Isle patterns.
Double Bed: This is a knitting machine with 2 beds of needles, usually for ribbing. It creates knit and purl stitches in a single row.
Main bed: The single needle bed that has patterning capabilities.

Ribber bed: The bed that, when put with a main bed, gives the ability to make knit and purl stitches on the same row and is often used to make "cuffs" and "collars" on garments.
Strippers: Some double bed knitting machines knit without weights. A patented Stripper System pushes the stitches off the needles as they are knit. This is opposed to a weight dependent system that pulls the knitting away from the needles
Lock: This is the mechanism that causes the needles to knit, slip or tuck as it passes over the needle bed.
Carriage: The part that passes the yarn back and forth over the needles.
Cam Box: This is the same thing as a Lock or carriage.
Bobbles: Is a technique to knit dimensional ½ balls.
Cables: Is a technique that "twists" yarn over each other.
Schematics: The drawings of garment shapes that are used to help a knitter see the individual parts of a garment.
Shaping features: Knitting machines use a number of ways to help you create the desired shape of a knitted piece. There are software programs that use a PC to design a shape and electronically transmit the information to the knitting machine.

Basic Functions:

Common to all knitting machines is needle position. At the end on each knitting bed you will notice the letters A, B, D, E. Needle position provides a way to divide your needles so that some stitches knit and others create a pattern or shape to your knitted fabric.

The carriage controls the needle position through the use of a selection mechanism called levers. These levers are found on both knitting carriages. It is through the action of the levers that needle position is converted to a specific type of stitch such as stockinet, Fair Isle, slip and tuck.

A Position

Out of Work Position or Rest Position.
These needles stay in this position when they are not used in your knitting.

B Position

Work Position. This is a universal needle position to both knitting beds. While knitting with either carriage, it is in this position that the needles return to when the side levers and hold levers are not engaged or working.

D Position

Upper Working Position is a pattern position used when knitting with punch cards. The needles are automatically returned to this position as the carriage moves across the needles in B or D position.

E Position

Hold Position. It is in this position that stitches on both needle beds are not knitted while the Hold Levers on the knitting carriage are engaged or in = position. This position is often used while knitting in pattern and for shaping your knitting. This needle position is universal to both knitting beds.

NOTES

PART 2

Let's Knit !!!...................
..................swatches

LET THE FUN BEGIN!

The cartridge, cam, controls, tension

This will be a very quick chapter. You will need to go through YOUR manual and get accustomed to the knobs and levers. Their abbreviations are in the previous chapters, but don't get nervous, it's actually easier to understand them while we USE them.

As you go to the following sections, we will be making swatches with the stockinette stitch. All this means is to move the carriage back and forth without any further manipulation. While you watch your work grow, you are looking at the BACK (the purl) of the work. As you bind off and look closer, notice the KNIT side as the front, and the PURL side as the back. This may seem VERY basic, but as you start using punch cards and get involved with hand manipulation and multiple colors, you need to remember you are looking at the back, and to occasionally check the front.

Swatches

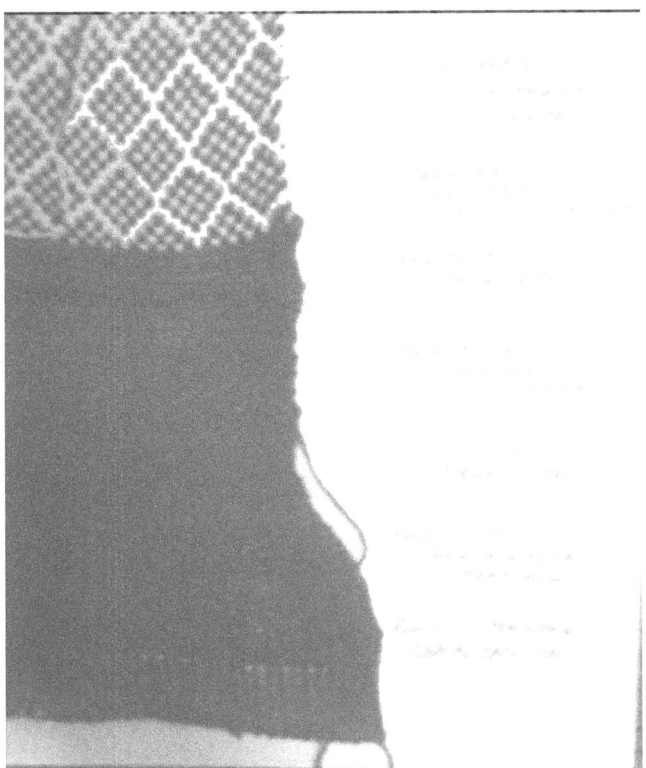

As you practice there are plenty of pages to keep track of your swatches.

I come back to my swatches often. When I first started, I never took note of what I had knitted. Be sure to leave lots of notes such as:
Name of yarn
Color
Washable?
Tension
Punch card #

Your book will grow, and the notes will be invaluable.

Casting on

Check your manual for instructions for your machine.

You Tube is excellent for visuals. Enter a search for Machine Knitting cast on and watch how easy it is. You can see many cast on and bind off techniques demonstrated on YouTube. Diana Sullivan from Austin, Texas, (Dianaknits) and Roberta Kelley have excellent video demonstrations.

Use your manual to thread the machine.

Start with COR (carriage on the right)
Cast on with equal amount of stitches R and L from zero.
I usually cast on 40. (20R and 20L)

The simple cast on

Move your Carriage to the right of the needle. Push all the needles to the A position (positions are marked on each side of the needle bed). Click your weaving brush levers into the up position.

Pull your working needles to the B position. Now push alternate needles to position E (all the way out). Pull your pre threaded yarn from under the K-Carriage, across the E needles, resting it in front of the bed but behind the hooks of the needles

Hanging on to the end off the yarn, slide the carriage from right to left, slowly, but firmly. It will feel a bit tight.

Move the carriage back to the right and put on your cast on comb, also adding some weights.

Return the weaving brush levers to the down position, and knit a few more rows.

THE SIMPLE CAST ON RAVELS, AND IS NOT USED FOR PERMANENT EDGES.
MAINLY USED FOR SCRAP ROWS .

The Simple cast on Swatch

The "e wrap" cast on

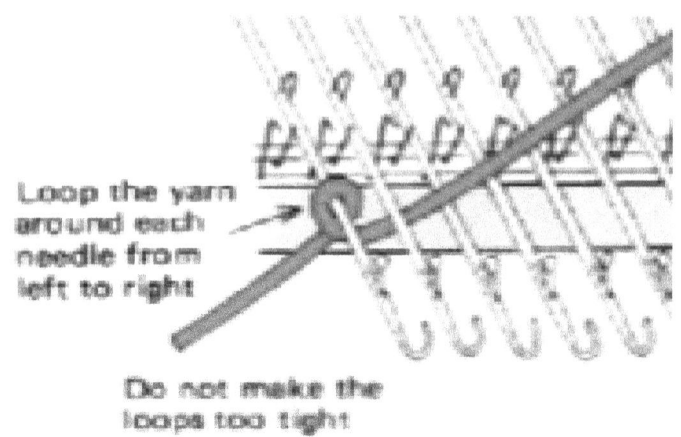

Loop the yarn around each needle from left to right

Do not make the loops too tight

Bring out the number of needles you need for the swatch. Hold the yarn between the first 2 needles on the left.

Start with the needle on the left. Hold 1 end of the yarn with your left hand, and use your right hand to wrap the yarn around the 1st needle. Wrap the yarn counterclockwise. Bring the yarn under the next needle and wrap it around again counterclockwise.

Repeat these steps across the row until you reach the last needle by the carriage. Hang the cast-on comb . Return the yarn inside the gate. Close the gate lever.

TIP: Make sure you do not catch your yarn at the end (carriage side) while hanging the cast on comb.

The "e-wrap" cast on Swatch

The "chain stitch" cast on

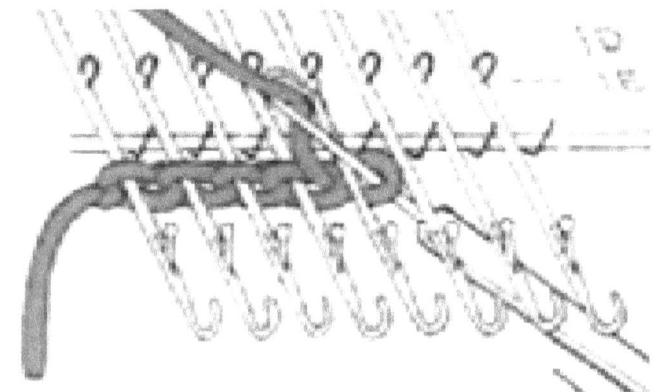

Take your yarn and make a slip knot at the end. Put that in the end of your latch tool.

Give it slight tension and come in between your 1st and 2nd needles on the left. Hold the yarn on the left and above the 1st needle. Use your latch tool to catch the yarn and pull down thru the loop.

The latch tool stays below, the strand of yarn stays above. Bring the latch tool between the next needle, up to the yarn, catch and pull thru. Repeat to the end, putting the last loop on the last needle. You are creating a chain stitch over all of your needles. Hang cast on comb.

TIP: Make sure you do not catch your yarn at the end (carriage side) while hanging the cast on comb.

The Chain Stitch cast on Swatch

Binding off

The latch hook cast off is neat and easy, and can be adjusted to any tension by knitting the last row at a looser tension, or by moving the needles back by hand.

With the latch hook, catch the first loop and lift off the needle. Pick up the next loop and bring it thru. Pick up the 3rd and bring it thru, continuing to the end. You will create a beautiful chain stitch bind off. Be careful you do not pull too tight.

Tapestry needle. Thread the tapestry needle with the tail yarn. You should have at least 3 lengths of tail.

Starting at the side with the tail, insert the needle into the 2nd loop, then the 1st loop, pull yarn through. Then enter the needle into the 3rd loop, then the 2nd, pull yarn through. Repeat with 4th and 3rd, 5th and 4th, etc, to the end. When you are at the end, insert the needle into the last loop, pull through and release work from machine.

Punch cards

Punch cards can be so much fun. You can use one punch card to easily make 5 (or more) completely different looking sweaters. All you need to do it change your lever positions. Check your manual for the correct positions for tuck, slip, fair isle and part. Create a swatch with each position. Then create a 2nd swatch with two colors…….. be sure to mark the punch card number and what position/tension you used on your swatch.

Hopefully your machine came with some cards to start with. You can also create your own. Before you buy blank cards, make sure you know if you need 12 or 24 hole cards. Here are some great resources.

If you are looking for cards, try here:
http://mypollywogs.com/knittingmachine.html
also ebay and etsy.

If you want to make your own, try here:
http://www.aboutknittingmachines.com/FreePunchCardPatterns.php

Troubleshooting

Also refer to your manual

I have found that because the knitting machine is actually a simple working machine. If there is a problem, usually it is time to be cleaned. Dust and yarn lint will build up and cause all kinds of frustrating situations. A good vacuum and lubrication wiped on with a soft cloth does wonders. Be sure to check the carriage and tension knobs. If further problems persist, check for bent or non-working needles. With a bit of patience, you can do most maintenance yourself.

Here are some common problems. and fixes….

Loops at the side of the knitting Tension mast too loose/ tension wire springs back too high Tighten the tension mast until the yarn is just gripped

Loops at the side of the knitting with very fine yarns Tension mast too loose (even if already at maximum) Try wrapping the yarn around the tension mast again to increase the tension

End stitches are pulling tight or raveling. Tension mast too tight/ tension wire pulling down towards carriage. Loosen the tension mast until the yarn is just gripped (towards the minus sign on Japanese machines)

Stitches dropping in same places every time Damaged needle Replace needle

Stitches dropping in random places. Flat needle retainer bar. Replace needle retainer bar with a new one.

Stitchesdropped at side. Taking carriage too far. Stop carriage movement immediately after hearing "click" at end of row

Squealing or screeching noise when moving carriage, sometimes worse in one direction. Carriage can also jam. Static/fluff build up. Clean underside of carriage and bed surface with a brush, apply a small amount of oil to back rail on bed and to hinges on underside of carriage. This happens more with fluffy and handknitting (not oiled/waxed) yarns. Try running them over a white non-scented candle when winding into a ball. You might also try hydrating the yarn overnight in the freezer or lightly dampening it with a spray bottle of water. Other suggestions: wipe the machine bed with a dryer sheet, earth it with a thin metal wire (I use a scourer), get a humidifier for the knitting room.

Yarn builds up on gate pegs —Add weights.

MORE RESOURCES

Free Patterns:

http://www.lionbrand.com/cgi-bin/patternIndex.fcgi?s=Machine
http://knittsings.com/free-knitting-machine-patterns/
http://www.freeknitpatterns.com/
http://www.aboutknittingmachines.com/
http://www.machine-knitting.net/machineknittingnet/machine-knitting-patterns-free/

Here is a monthly magazine, a bit pricey, but you can order one issue at a time to check it out before you decide to subscribe:
http://machineknittingmonthlyusa.net/machineknittingmonthly.html

Free Charts
http://www.knitting-and.com/knitting/patterns-charts.htm
http://erssieknits.squarespace.com/knitting-charts/
http://www.tricksyknitter.com/knitting-chart-maker/shared-charts/

…and more great youtube videos:

Using Hand Knitting Patterns for Machine Knitting
https://www.youtube.com/watch?v=apjhZcAGvrM
What to consider when deciding to machine knit a hand knit pattern, and how to go about it.

Hand Knit Terms for Machine Knitters
https://www.youtube.com/watch?v=ITak20dYJeY
Shows how to accomplish hand knitting terms on a knitting machine.

Pintucks for Machine Knitters
https://www.youtube.com/watch?v=csw9ycgslvs
Interesting technique....

Great apps to check out:

Design your own cardigan
http://knitting.bikibird.com/Cardigan/CardiganForm.php
http://pattern-knit.com/calculator.php
http://www.jimmybeanswool.com/secure-html/onlineec/knittingCalculator.asp
http://www.knittingfool.com/SweaterPatterns/SweaterWheel.aspx
http://frenchroastdesign.com/armscye/

Increase, decrease, bust darts, more.
http://www.thedietdiary.com/knittingfiend/tools/

Waist shaper:
http://www.knittingdaily.com/blogs/daily/archive/2008/03/27/new-online-knitting-tool_3A00_-waist-shaping-calculator.aspx

Taper sleeves
http://blog.knititnow.com/post.cfm/knitting-magic-formula

Design your own punch card:
http://knitting.bikibird.com/jacquardform.html

How about your "best friend"
http://www.thedietdiary.com/cgibin/chart_dog.pl

Happy Knitting

SWATCHES

SWATCHES

SWATCHES

Lightning Source UK Ltd.
Milton Keynes UK
UKHW03f0609060718
325319UK00004B/274/P